LOOKING EAST

STAIRS

Greene&Greene for Kids

Greene & Greene for Kids

ART • ARCHITECTURE • ACTIVITIES

KATHLEEN THORNE-THOMSEN

Gibbs Smith, Publisher
Salt Lake City

First Edition
08 07 06 05 04   5 4 3 2 1
Text © 2004 Kathleen Thorne-Thomsen
Photographs © 2004 as noted throughout

Library of Congress Control Number: 2004107723

Published by
Gibbs Smith, Publisher
P.O. Box 667
Layton, Utah 84041

Orders: 1.800.748.5439
www.gibbs-smith.com

ISBN 1-58685-440-2

Designed by Kathleen Thorne-Thomsen
Drawings (owl and sweet pea) by Charles Greene
Printed in Hong Kong

Disclaimer: The author and the publisher bear no
responsibility or liability for injuries or property damage
that may occur from using the information or participating
in the activities contained in this book.

For Astrid Ellersieck

and Tom Heinz, Randell Makinson, and Paul Rocheleau. With thanks to Lyn Adelstein, Peggy Park Bernal, Tom Blum, Paul Bockhorst, Edward Bosley, Julia Bosley, Erin Chase, Andre Chaves, Ann Chaves, Simone Chaves, Susan DiCicco, Kennedy Dinius, Riley Dinius, Everardo Farias, Mark Fiennes, Renee Guilbault, Virginia Dart Greene Hales, Doreen Hambleton, Jan Hurff, Wendy Hurff, Natalie Howard, Howard Isham, Molly Isham, Ben Ipekjian, David Judson, Brad Macneil, Chris Martin, Robena Mapstone, Carrie McDade, Kevin McCafferty, George McDonald, Viola McDonald, Dan McLoughlin, Chistopher Molinar, Bill Moses and family, Alicia Mulliken, Gene Oster, Lauralee Oster, Lian Partlow, Dorothea Paul, June Poust, Graham Pulliam, James G. Pulliam, James J. Pulliam, Elaine Rocheleau, Joss Rodgers, Jessica Roquette, Ann Scheid, Sherri Schottlaender, Kristin Standaert, Chad Taylor, Christine Wheeler, Ardis Willwerth, Mary Jo Winder, and Robert Winter.

Activities

A Note to Parents, Teachers, and Grandparents

Architecture and the design of houses are fundamentally interesting subjects to children. Is this because the spaces that we inhabit seem so familiar and yet endlessly mysterious? Old houses in particular hold a special fascination for children, and the exquisite architecture of Charles and Henry Greene—with its tactile, craft-oriented details and supremely aesthetic decorative overlays—ranks high in providing an ideal historical and visual narrative to engage a young audience on the subject of architecture.

The work of Greene & Greene includes some of the most revered American home designs of the early twentieth century and their houses have fascinated adults and children alike, especially since the opening of The Gamble House to the public in 1966. In cooperation with the Pasadena Unified School District and the University of Southern California School of Architecture, The Gamble House has for more than two decades arranged tours for thousands of local elementary school children. These tours are unusual because they are conducted by middle school students only a few years older than their visitors. Junior docents, as they are known, are specially trained to discuss with their young charges the story of the house and its design in a way that kids can appreciate and learn from.

While many of us live in old houses, they tend to be far less pedigreed than The Gamble House. Exceptional examples of buildings and their interiors, however, can teach much about the appreciation of the more ordinary things that surround us in our own homes and furnishings, be they built-in cupboards or a simple fireplace. Now *Greene & Greene for Kids,* authored by Kathleen Thorne-Thomsen, whose book *Frank Lloyd Wright for Kids* has sold more than 35,000 copies, brings to life for children the historic architecture of this gifted fraternal team. Through this accessible and engaging text, evocative and whimsical illustrations, and numerous fun activities, astute teachers, parents, and grandparents will recognize how easily the basic ideas behind architecture—along with the unique challenges of home life of a century ago—can make for a vivid and stimulating learning experience for the young reader.

Edward R. Bosley
James N. Gamble, Director
The Gamble House, Pasadena
University of Southern California School of Architecture

This painting shows what Cincinnati, Ohio, looked like when Charlie and Hallie were born. The artist painted a forest, farmlands, the Ohio River, steamboats and barges, and the city. Do you notice the black smoke hanging over the city? The smoke is from factories and homes that burned wood and coal for heat.

Cincinnati, Ohio

Cincinnati is a city on the banks of the Ohio River. Before the Civil War, it was a good place to live because men could easily find jobs at Cincinnati's river port. But when the Civil War began in 1861, river shipping practically came to a stop because of the fighting.

Many new railroad lines were built after the Civil War. Because it was now easier to ship goods by train, Cincinnati's river port was not as busy as it had been. Cincinnati was still a good place to live because manufacturing companies like Procter & Gamble provided jobs and people could make a good living.

The Greenes were one of the many young families living in Cincinnati after the Civil War. Thomas Sumner Greene returned home to the city in 1866 after serving in the Union Army. He married a young woman named Lelia Mather. Lelia had grown up near Cincinnati, on a large farm in West Virginia.

Thomas and Lelia's first son, Charles, was born on October 12, 1868. They nicknamed him Charlie. A brother, Henry, was born the following year on January 23, 1869. His nickname was Hallie. The Greene family lived near the large Procter & Gamble factory. Who would have guessed that one day Charlie and Hallie would design a very famous house for the Gamble family in faraway Pasadena, California?

This is Charlie.

This is Hallie.

Were Soap and Candles Important?

When Charlie and Hallie were young boys, families made their own soap and candles. This was done outside because both candles and soap were made with tallow. Tallow is a very smelly oil made by cooking animal fat for a long time. Soap and candles that are made from tallow are brown and strong smelling.

Soap was important because it helped to wash away dirt and germs. Although doctors didn't know as much then as they do now, they did recognize that soap killed germs that make people sick.

Candles were important because there were no electric lights. Cincinnati's average families used kerosene lamps and candles to light their homes. If not properly tended, these lights could easily start a fire. Using them was dangerous, but it was better than living in the dark.

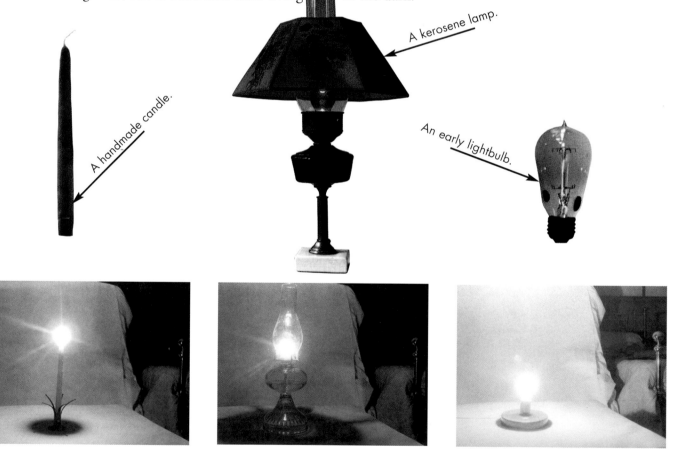

A handmade candle.

A kerosene lamp.

An early lightbulb.

These photographs were taken in a dark room at night. The film was exposed to the light for exactly the same length of time. The pictures show the amount of light given off by a candle (far left), a kerosene lamp (middle), and a lightbulb (far right).

Procter & Gamble

In this illustration, advertising Ivory as the soap that floats, a toy kitten is shown floating on a bar of Ivory soap.

James Gamble was an Irish immigrant who settled in Cincinnati and learned to make soap. He met a candle maker named William Procter when he married into William's family. Since both candles and soap are made from tallow, it made sense for James and William to work together. That is how the Procter & Gamble Company began in 1837.

William and James collected waste materials, tallow, and wood ashes from Cincinnati's households and used them to manufacture soap and candles. It was a good system: Procter & Gamble had a steady supply of ingredients and the families of Cincinnati had the convenience of ready-made soap and candles.

Soon salesmen were selling Procter & Gamble's products outside Cincinnati. In fact, during the Civil War, the company won a contract from the government to supply soap and candles to soldiers in the Union Army. By the time Charlie and Hallie were born, Procter & Gamble was a very successful Cincinnati business.

In 1879, a mistake happened in the soap factory. As the story goes, a worker was making a batch of white soap. When it was time for lunch, he forgot to turn off the soap-mixing machine. After lunch, the worker noticed that the soap looked a little different. He wondered if he would have to throw it away. Procter & Gamble was thrifty, and so the soap was packaged and sold.

Soon customers wrote to the Procter & Gamble Company asking for more "floating soap." It was then that the discovery was made: overmixing added extra air to the soap. And since air is lighter than water, overmixed soap floats in water.

Procter & Gamble's business boomed. Twenty-eight years later, in California, the money from Ivory Soap would pay to build the Gamble House, one of Charlie and Hallie's finest homes.

LESSON NO. 22 A BADGER CHARM BY MARGARET J. POSTGATE

Ivory Soap Sculpture

FINISHED MODEL

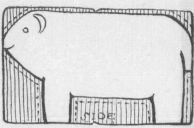

SIDE

THE Zuni Indians who live in New Mexico chose certain animals to represent the points of the compass, the seasons, the color and the elements. They carved small charms of these animals out of stone.

Here is the badger, "who," these Indians said, "digs his hole on the sunny side of the hills, and in the winter appears only when the sun shines warm above him; who digs among the roots of the juniper and the cedar, from which fire is kindled with the fire drill, to find the wild tobacco which grows only where the fire has burned."

So the Zunis picked the badger to stand for the *South, Summer,* the color *red,* and the element *fire.*

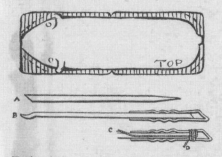

TOP

Tools—A large cake of Ivory Soap. Pen knife or paring knife. One orange stick with one blade and one pointed end (wooden tool A). One orange stick to which a hairpin is tied as shown in B, C, D; file bent end of hairpin to a sharp knife edge (wire tool).

Directions:

With point of wooden tool draw badger on sides of soap.

Then with knife cut away soap up to dotted lines.

Do the same with top, front and back.

With wire tool or blade end of wooden tool, shave or carve down to the actual form of badger.

Work slowly, turn model often and compare it with drawing.

Eyes, ears, mouth and tail should be put in last with point of wooden tool.

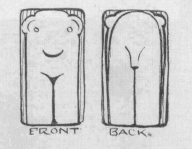

FRONT BACK

Remember—Save the chips and shavings from your carving and give them to your mother to use in kitchen or laundry. And remember too, after a hard practice at football or basketball, nothing makes you feel better than a good Ivory all-over-bath—hair and everything. Ivory is white and clean and it makes a gorgeous lather. And you can always find it in the tub—because—*it floats!*

PROCTER & GAMBLE

IVORY SOAP

99⁴⁴/₁₀₀% Pure —IT FLOATS!

© 1926 P. & G. Co.

St. Nicholas was a popular children's magazine. It was published from 1873, when Charlie was 5 years old and Hallie was 4, until the mid-1900s. Some of America's best writers including Mark Twain, Louisa May Alcott, and L. Frank Baum wrote stories for *St. Nicholas.* Here is a soap sculpture craft from the November 1926 issue.

Ivory Soap Sculpture

Materials

1 package of 4 bath-size bars of Ivory soap

A dinner knife with a dull, thin blade or a plastic knife

Useful Tools

▲ A wooden toothpick for carving out eyes and other small areas

● An orange stick or other manicure tools (purchased at a cosmetics store)

■ A large bobby pin

● Dental floss to tie the bobby pin to the orange stick

● Several pieces of waxed paper

Ask an adult to help you choose a knife. You may follow the instructions for carving the Zuni badger on page 6 or you can create an animal from your own imagination. Ivory soap is very soft and easy to carve—you may want to practice carving on a test bar of soap before beginning your project. To prevent breaking the soap, shave off or cut away only a few small pieces at a time. The soap shavings may be saved and used in the washing machine later.

Growing Up

Charlie and Hallie's mother often took them on a boat ride to visit her family's farm in West Virginia. Living on the Mather farm taught the boys about nature and living in the country. The Mather farm was nearly self-sufficient. This means that the Mather family built their own house and grew or made everything else they needed, including food, soap, candles, cloth, furniture, tools, wagons, and barns.

The farm family built their own house.

The stove and pots and pans were probably not made by the farm family.

The farm family grew and made all of their food.

The farm family made all of their clothes.

The farm family made tables, chairs, beds—all of their furniture.

The farm family made their rugs.

The family cat worked, too. She kept the barn free of mice.

Thomas Sumner Greene wanted his sons to be architects. He thought they should learn to work together so they could be partners in their own architecture business one day. To encourage them, he told stories about his grandfather who had been an important architect. When Charlie was eight, his father bought him a book, *Routledges Boys' Book of Trades,* about architecture and building.

Lelia Mather Greene did not quite agree with her husband. She wanted her sons to be artists. Lelia loved to paint designs on china and sometimes made a little extra money for the family by selling her work. She shared her interest with her sons. She gave Charlie and Hallie drawing and painting supplies and encouraged them to draw.

This is the book Thomas Greene gave Charlie when he was eight.

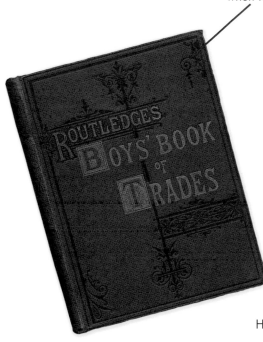

Lelia Greene gave her sons art supplies that might have looked like this box of paints and the charcoal pencils.

Here is a hand-painted china plate. Do you think Lelia painted scenes from nature?

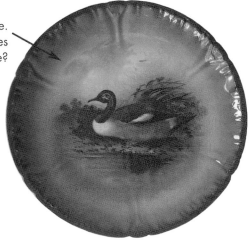

Charcoal pencils.

9

A New Home

When Charlie was six and Hallie was five, the Greene family moved to St. Louis. They lived in a row house. Thomas Greene rented a house at the end because it had more light and better air circulation, and because there were windows on three sides instead of two.

Not long after the family moved to St. Louis, Thomas Greene decided to become a doctor. He wanted to help people and he wanted a profession that would pay him more money. He was interested in catarrh, or illnesses that cause a runny nose. The smoky city air must have caused a lot of runny noses. Thomas Greene moved back to Cincinnati for four years while he attended medical school. Lelia Greene took Charlie and Hallie to live on the Mather farm in West Virginia. The boys must have missed their father!

These large tanks held water for the row houses.

Windows.

A horse-drawn trolley.

Horse.

This is a row house in Cincinnati. The Greenes lived here. Row houses share walls on two sides. This picture is fuzzy because the original photograph was made using a very old photography technique. See page 100.

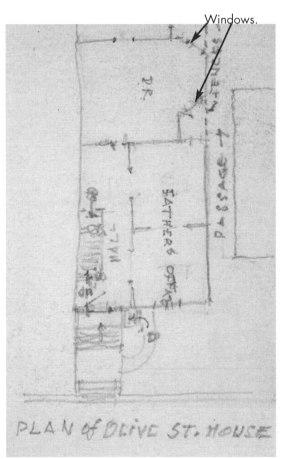

PLAN of OLIVE ST. HOUSE

Hallie drew a picture of the first floor of the Greene's row house. We can see a hall, his father's office, and a dining room with windows. There is a narrow passage and then another building with more row houses.

What Was America Like?

In 1876, the United States of America celebrated its 100th birthday. Large numbers of people were moving to cities where they could find work.

Cities were not healthy places to live. They were crowded and dirty. Streets were filled with garbage, and rivers were filled with sewage. The air was hazy with smoke and soot from coal fires and factory waste. Drinking water was full of bacteria and often made city people very sick. People traveled by horseback or mule, in carriages and wagons pulled by animals, or by boat or train.

Food for the average American was bread and vegetables. Vegetables were plentiful in the late summer months, but the rest of the year only vegetables that grow underground—potatoes, carrots, beets, and onions—were available. Families rarely had fresh meat or fish. They ate dried, smoked, or salted fish or meat whenever they could afford it. Cucumber pickles were a special treat in wintertime. The Heinz Company began selling catsup in 1876. Catsup was a treat—a tasty addition to an otherwise dull diet.

Electricity was a new discovery. It was rarely used to produce light because the lightbulb wasn't invented until 1879. It was very dark at night because homes were lit with candles, kerosene lamps, and fireplaces. Wealthier homes had gaslights that burned with a hissing sound and produced a dim light. Waste from these lights often made it as hazy inside as it was outside.

There were many house fires in the city. When a fire started, the house usually burned to the ground. It took firemen a long time to get to the fire in heavy horse-drawn wagons. They had to carry their water with them.

There was no hot running water and in many cases no running water at all. Water had to be carried into the house in buckets, and sometimes the dirty used water had to be carried back outside in buckets. Some homes had hand pumps in the kitchen sink. The more modern homes had a water tank on the roof of the house that allowed cold water to run into a sink.

There were few indoor toilets. Some rich people had them, but since no one knew how to ventilate the sewer gas that escapes from a toilet, houses with indoor toilets smelled very bad! Most people used a small wooden outhouse in the yard. In the outhouse, the waste settled into an open hole in the ground. Smelly!

A backyard outhouse.

11

Kitchen stoves were heated with fires made from wood or coal. The family bathtub was often found right next to the kitchen stove so that water could be heated easily and poured into the tub. Many bathtubs had fancy claw-feet to make them look more like the furniture.

Alexander Graham Bell's telephone, and Thomas Alva Edison's phonograph and electric lightbulb were exciting new inventions. But not many people could afford them.

Most city streets had gaslights if they had any lights at all. Gaslights were dim and they had to be lit by hand every night and then extinguished by hand again in the morning. City streets were unpaved. They were dusty, muddy, and full of ruts and animal waste. New York City was an exception. A few streets in New York were paved.

Women could not vote and they did not earn much money. Most women did not have jobs outside the home.

Bicycles appeared in the United States after the Civil War and soon became a national craze because they gave people freedom to move around. The first bicycles cost the average working man six months' pay. Early motor vehicles (cars) also appeared at this time. They were powered by steam, gas, or electricity and ran at a top speed of six miles per hour.

A telephone.

Americans were reading two new books by Mark Twain: *The Adventures of Tom Sawyer* and *The Adventures of Huckleberry Finn*.

Families entertained themselves by making their own music—everyone learned to sing or play an instrument—and by telling stories or reading to each other. Old and young often did handwork like sewing, knitting, carving, carpentry, or quilting. Winter nights seemed very long because it was so hard to see at night. City people attended live plays, concerts, and circus shows when they could afford the price of a ticket.

Perhaps the most popular form of entertainment, next to the circus, was the fair. There were fairs of all sizes: local county fairs, state fairs, and even huge world's fairs. A famous world's fair was held in Philadelphia in 1876. It was called the Centennial Exposition because it celebrated the 100th birthday of the United States. Countries from all over the world exhibited at this fair.

This is a mandolin.

Food for Kids

In these days children had many new and delicious foods to eat. Many of these foods are the same as those enjoyed by children today—hot dogs, hamburgers, ice cream treats, and sweet fizzy drinks. When Charlie and Hallie were young these treats were very new.

Nancy Johnson invented the hand-cranked ice cream maker in 1843. It worked something like a butter churn surrounded by ice. Everyone wanted ice cream but it could not be stored at home because there were no home refrigerators. Special stores that sold ice cream, called soda fountains, sprang up everywhere. Children went to soda fountains for a dish of ice cream.

Two cities claim credit for creating the first ice cream sundae: Buffalo, New York, and Two Rivers, Wisconsin. A sundae is a dish of ice cream with chocolate or cherry syrup poured on top. Tradition says that this ice cream treat was named a "sundae" because the extra cost of the syrup made it too expensive to eat except as a "Sunday" treat.

Robert Green takes credit for creating the first chocolate soda. At his soda fountain, Robert Green sold a popular drink that was a mixture of milk, soda water, and chocolate flavoring. One day he ran out of milk and used ice cream instead, hoping his customers wouldn't notice the difference. The sales at Green's soda fountain climbed from $6 per day to $600 per day. Do you think his customers noticed?

A soda fountain in a drugstore.

Hires Root Beer, one of America's oldest soft drinks, was the creation of a Philadelphia pharmacist named Charles E. Hires. At first, Mr. Hires sold his mixture of roots, berries, and herbs as a tea that could be brewed at home. Then a bubbly version of the Hires root tea appeared in 1876 at Philadelphia's Centennial Exposition. Everyone loved it. Root beer became a favorite American drink. People brewed and bottled root beer at home. Some bought packages of roots; others went to the local woods and dug up the roots themselves. The bubbles came from yeast, the same ingredient used to raise bread. One old recipe recommends making the root beer in warm weather so the yeast will ferment and make bubbles faster. Sometimes the yeast made too many bubbles and the corks blew off the bottles with a loud pop!

Old-Fashioned Ice Cream Soda

1/4 cup milk
3 tablespoons chocolate syrup
2 scoops of vanilla or chocolate ice cream
1 cup cold club soda

Pour milk in a large, cold glass. Stir in the chocolate syrup. Add one scoop of ice cream and 1/4 cup of club soda. Mash the ice cream a little and stir to mix. Add the remaining ice cream and soda. Stir to mix and serve at once with a straw and a long-handled spoon.

Old-Fashioned Root Beer Float

1 bottle old-fashioned root beer
2 scoops of vanilla ice cream

Pour a little root beer in a tall chilled glass. Add 2 scoops of vanilla ice cream. Fill glass with root beer. Serve at once with a straw and a long-handled spoon.

14

What Were Manual Training Schools?

Manual training schools teach students to work with their hands. After the Civil War, there was a shortage of workers because a lot of American men were killed on the battlefields. Manual Training Schools were developed to train skilled workers. At the same time, America's factories needed more workers to produce goods such as clothing and furniture for a growing population.

In a manual training school, traditional academic subjects like math, science, and English were combined with handwork classes like woodworking, mechanical drawing, and machine shop. The idea was this: Training the hand to work with the eye in woodworking or metal shop improved a student's ability to concentrate and learn math, science, and English. A motto that fit these schools was "educating the mind through hand and heart." Another way to say it might be "through hand and art."

Manual training classes spread all around the country. These boys are working in a school class in 1910. Do you notice that three of the boys are barefoot?

The Manual Training School of Washington University

It was good fortune for Charlie and Hallie that the first manual training school—The Manual Training School of Washington University—was in St. Louis. Dr. Greene wanted his sons to attend and he could afford to send them there because he had a successful practice treating patients with breathing problems.

These three-sided bay windows let more light and air into the house.

There are two small figures peeking out the window. Do you think that Charlie and Hallie were watching the photographer take a picture of their parents?

Dr. Greene.

Mrs. Greene.

The Greene family could afford a large house with more natural light. This house had open space all around it which allowed air to circulate through the house. How different it is from the Greenes' row house in Cincinnati!

Charlie enrolled at the Manual Training School when he was fifteen, and Hallie followed a year later. In school their time was divided equally between English, mathematics, Latin, history, science, mechanical drawing, and wood, metal, or machine shop. All of the subjects they studied prepared them to be architects. Charlie's grades varied. He got 100 percent in freehand drawing and a zero in penmanship. It would seem that if you had skill in drawing it would have some effect on your penmanship, but in Charlie's case it didn't. (Or maybe he just didn't turn in his penmanship assignments.) Hallie's grades were much better. He obviously enjoyed the school and later said that his success was due to the time he spent there.

This is one of Charlie's report cards.

MANUAL TRAINING SCHOOL,
WASHINGTON UNIVERSITY.
REPORT of the Standing

of *Chas Greene* of the *Junior* Year Class,

for the five weeks ending *May 7th* 188_

This is Hallie.

This is Charlie.

What Did Charlie and Hallie Learn in College?

Charlie graduated from The Manual Training School of Washington University a year before Hallie. He wanted to be an artist, not an architect, but Dr. Greene had a different plan for him. He found Charlie work as an apprentice* in a local architect's office. When Hallie graduated from the Manual Training School, Dr. Greene sent the boys to Boston to take a two-year course in architecture at the Massachusetts Institute of Technology.

Two years seems like a very short time when compared to five years, which is what it takes to earn a degree in architecture today. But in the late 1800s, it was possible for people to call themselves architects and not have studied architecture at all. Frank Lloyd Wright, who worked at the same time as Charles and Henry Greene, is an example of a successful architect who never studied architecture in school.

Boston's Massachusetts Institute of Technology, or MIT, was the first American school to offer a degree in architecture. But it was not the best in the world. That distinction was reserved for the famous Ecole des Beaux-Arts in Paris, France. American men (and one woman, Julia Morgan) who could afford it studied architecture in Paris.

Students at the Ecole des Beaux-Arts (ā cole day bows-ar) were taught classical European-style architecture. They learned to design enormous public buildings using geometric shapes, columns, and classical** decorations. Examples of the beaux-arts style may be seen in older American public buildings. The United States Capitol in Washington, D.C., is a fine example of beaux-arts architecture. Professors who had studied at the Ecole des Beaux-Arts taught students at MIT in the same design tradition.

> *apprentice
>
> An apprentice is a student who works for someone who is skilled in a trade in order to learn the trade.

> **classical
>
> Classical decorations are taken from ancient Greek and Roman architecture.

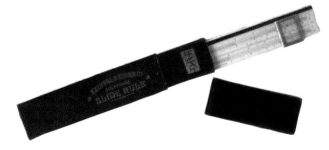

This is Hallie's slide rule. Before computers, slide rules were used for math calculations.

A beaux-arts style building in Paris.

At MIT, Charlie and Hallie (now old enough to be called Charles and Henry) had a choice of architecture programs—either two years for a certificate or four years for a degree. They qualified for the shorter two-year course. Two-year students studied drawing, sketching, and spatial composition* as they worked to develop design skills. They also took classes in basic math, geometry, either French or German, and the history of fine art.

*spatial composition

Designs that had depth as well as length and width.

In the late 1800s, there were two different ideas or theories about architecture in the United States. The first theory was patterned after the classical style of the Ecole des Beaux-Arts. Students of this kind of architecture studied buildings that had been built in Europe in the past and used these designs to create new buildings.

The second theory about architecture came from the writings of an Englishman named John Ruskin. Ruskin said that an architect should first learn how to build using the hand tools traditional to the art of building. Ruskin also believed that architects should learn the science and history of architecture.

The Greenes understood both of these theories about architecture. They had learned the science and the craft of building in the woodworking and machine shops of the Manual Training School in St. Louis, and they had learned the classical and historical approach to architecture at MIT.

After graduating from MIT's two-year course, Charles and Henry stayed on in Boston. It was an exciting city! They were exposed to a rich cultural life. They witnessed the construction of the Boston Public Library and sometimes went to Trinity Church on Copley Square. They lived only a short block from these places and from Boston's Museum of Fine Arts. They absorbed the details of architect Henry Hobson Richardson's unique style while they worked for several Boston architects who had been influenced by him. In their free time, they traveled outside Boston to visit relatives and friends.

Columns with classical decorations.

Henry Hobson Richardson

Henry Hobson Richardson was one of the first architects to put forth a new direction in American architecture. He combined classical European designs with his own unique vision. His work was bold, romantic, decorative, intense, and colorful. This represented a break with the classical beaux-arts style that was popular with America's other leading architects.

Richardson studied first at Harvard and then in Paris at the Ecole des Beaux-Arts. His style, which is now called Richardsonian Romanesque, featured heavy stone and brick walls. It had dramatic arches outlining the windows and doors, and decorative patterns in the brickwork. Richardson's famous Trinity Church was just a block away from the boardinghouse where Charles and Henry Greene lived while they were attending MIT. Although Charles and Henry never worked for Richardson (he died two years before they entered MIT), they worked as apprentices for several Boston architects who had worked for him.

This is a view of the Natural History Museum at the Woburn Public Library, in Woburn, Massachusetts. It is an example of the work of Henry Hobson Richardson.

21

A Journey to the West

While Charles and Henry were working in Boston, their parents were still living in St. Louis. Business was bad for Dr. Greene. He wasn't getting any new patients. Mrs. Greene was suffering from asthma. They even had to sell their house and move into smaller rented rooms. In 1892, Dr. and Mrs. Greene decided to move west. Dr. Greene would give his business a fresh start, and the clean air in Pasadena, California, would help Mrs. Greene's asthma.

Pasadena was a tiny new town just east of Los Angeles at the foot of the towering San Gabriel Mountains. People who wrote about Pasadena in those days remember that there was magic in the air. Winters were warm and sunny. Orchards of orange trees gave off the fragrant scent of blossoms, and snow sometimes dusted the nearby mountains. In spring, fields of bright orange poppies contrasted against the clear blue sky. Summers were dry and hot and it almost never rained. The air was clean and invigorating.

To the Greenes, who were used to dirty city air, Pasadena must have seemed like a paradise on earth. They wanted their sons to visit them so they could see all that Pasadena had to offer.

In 1893, the journey from Boston to California took almost a week. It had been five years since Charles and Henry had been at home with their parents. It must have been an exciting trip for them.

Picking Poppies at the Foothills of Pasadena, Cal.

A Stop in Chicago

The White City attracted many visitors.

On the way to Pasadena, Charles and Henry Greene stopped in Chicago to see the Columbian Exposition, a gigantic world's fair. The Columbian Exposition was competing with the 1889 Paris *Exposition Universelle Internationale,* the best fair the world had ever seen. The Eiffel Tower, the symbol of the *Exposition Universelle,* continues to this day as a monument to the city of Paris. Congress felt the United States had been outdone by the *Exposition Universelle.* They voted to hold an American fair in Chicago that would surpass the French fair. The fairgrounds were on the shore of Lake Michigan just south of downtown Chicago. The Columbian Exposition was nicknamed the White City.

The White City was an impressive site to see. It stood apart from the Black City—Chicago. Dark and dirty air hung over the Black City. It was polluted with noise, animal and human waste, garbage, and the gagging smell of Chicago's stockyards. In the Black City people were crowded together in unhealthy slum buildings. Many of them died from illnesses caused by drinking impure water.

23

For many visitors, a nighttime visit to the fair was their first view of electric lights. Do you notice how dark the fair was even with the electric lights because there were no lights from nearby Chicago? Can you imagine how dark city nights were then?

By contrast, the White City was spacious and clean. The drinking water was spring fed and pure. Huge beaux-arts buildings looked out over shimmering blue lagoons. All of the buildings were painted pure white. They sparkled against the lagoons and the deeper blue waters of Lake Michigan. At night the White City was lit with thousands of Thomas Edison's electric lightbulbs. First-time visitors to the White City were often overcome with emotion. They stood in silence and some had tears in their eyes. It was just that beautiful.

24

The world's first Ferris wheel towered over the midway—the central walkway of the fair. The Ferris wheel was so gigantic it could hold 2,160 people at one time. Do you think the giant Ferris wheel was more impressive than the Eiffel Tower?

The Eiffel Tower, symbol of the *Exposition Universelle Internationale,* Paris, France.

Landscape architect Frederick Law Olmstead and Chicago architect Daniel Burnham worked for more than three years to create the White City. They were helped by the best architects and designers in the United States. Thousands of laborers worked night and day to build the White City. The cost was very high. Burnham and Olmstead were able to create this masterpiece of American architecture because the City of Chicago and the federal government gave them money.

States, organizations, and countries from all around the world contributed exhibits to the fair. Japan sent three half-size models of temple buildings. This was the first time people from all around the world could view real Japanese timber construction. A fascinating bungalow village from the Malay Peninsula had open-air sleeping areas above the ground floor.

25

The Woman's Building was designed and furnished by women. Working together on the Woman's Building brought women from all over the country together and helped to set the Women's Suffrage movement—women's right to vote—in motion.

Just outside the fair grounds, Buffalo Bill set up his Wild West Show. It was so good that some early visitors to the fair thought the Wild West Show was the fair.

Although the White City has been gone more than one hundred years, it is a lasting memory for America. It was the beginning of the City Beautiful movement, which affects Americans even today. Just think about America's beautiful cities and the large number of public buildings that look like the buildings in the White City.

City Hall, Pasadena, California, 2004.

The Columbian Exposition, Chicago, 1893.

Design a Classical House

Materials

Scissors

1 piece of white board
(8 $\frac{1}{2}$ x 11 inches)

Glue stick

You can find drawings of columns, windows with shutters, a door, and a pediment on the website www.greeneandgreeneforkids.com. You can copy them to your computer's desktop. If you do not have access to a computer, you can trace the drawings on the next two pages.

Copy the drawings to your computer, then open the files and print several copies. Now you can cut them out and arrange them on the white board to create a beaux-arts house. Use the long side of the board for the base. When you have created a building that you like, glue the paper shapes in place with the glue stick.

This triangular shape is called a pediment. The pediment has decorative windows.

Ionic columns.

27

This house has a pediment, Ionic columns, and decorative panels. Is it a bungalow?

This decorative panel is also called a frieze.

A Corinthian column.

An Ionic column.

A pediment.

29

Where Do Great Architects Get Their Ideas?

Great architects are born with talent but they are also influenced by the world around them. They are influenced by parents, subjects taught in school, outstanding teachers, home and community, and how they see nature—including animals, plants, rocks, and colors.

These are pictures of Charlie and Hallie's parents when they were young.

Many of the students at the Manual Training School are holding tools.

This is Charlie.

In Pasadena

Charles and Henry didn't intend to stay in Pasadena. They wanted to visit their parents and then open their own architecture office in the Midwest. But Pasadena offered opportunities they might not easily find in Chicago or Kansas City. Charles and Henry's parents encouraged them to stay and open an architecture office, and they did.

Pasadena was a new city with a strong spirit. It was founded in 1886, just seven years before Charles and Henry's arrival. Residents had new ideas about making their community better. They believed in the importance of education, art, music, and literature, and Pasadena had a newspaper, a library, and public schools.

Pasadena was growing by leaps and bounds. It seemed that the population doubled every few years. Many newcomers were wealthy. They wanted large attractive homes of the best quality. When Charles and Henry arrived, Pasadena had only four architects. It made sense to open an office where there was a steady supply of new clients and a small number of trained architects.

BIRD'S EYE VIEW OF PASADENA, CAL.

Southern California had excellent local materials to build with. There were smooth gray river stones in all sizes that were easily found near a large natural *arroyo seco.** Lumber, including redwood and cedar, could be shipped from Northern California and Oregon. Local factories made bricks of the finest quality.

Pasadena's extraordinary geography provided a background for building fine homes. It had amazing views of the San Gabriel Mountains, the Arroyo Seco, and in the distance, the Pacific Ocean.

Many plants and trees grew in the warm climate. There were groves of orange and lemon trees and acres of grape vineyards. Gigantic old oak trees, sycamores, roses, wisteria, and flowers of every size and description grew freely. In fact, so many roses grew that some people didn't paint their houses. They simply planted roses that grew like weeds and covered the walls and sometimes even the roof of the house.

*arroyo seco
The Spanish words for "dry riverbed."

This Pasadena house looks like it is peeking out from behind a giant rose bush.

The Office of Architects Greene & Greene

In the architecture firm, each Greene brother had his own talent. Charles was an artist, a craftsman, and a dreamer. He was full of creative ideas. Henry, on the other hand, was a practical designer. He had a fine sense of space and proportion. Henry attended to details and was more exact and punctual than Charles. When it was necessary, Charles could duplicate Henry's strengths and Henry did the same for Charles. When they worked together, they did their best work.

Charles and Henry must have had some creative ideas about the houses

Henry Greene.

Charles Greene.

they would have liked to design. But they needed work, and to get work they had to please the people who would pay them. Those were their clients.

In 1894, Americans were not as willing to experiment with the design of their homes as they are now. Therefore the first houses designed by the office of Architects Greene & Greene did not look like the houses that later made them famous. The first houses used popular styles and decorative details that were also used by other American architects. These houses would have been just as happy in St. Louis, Cincinnati, or Boston. The dramatic change to a hot, dry, and sunny climate had not yet affected the Greenes' work. But in a few years, Charles and Henry would develop a unique style that was especially suited to the Southern California weather.

In 1895, the Greenes built the Willis Eason House. Even though it is a small house, the Eason House has some touches of the beaux-arts style that Charles and Henry had learned in Boston. The brothers may also have remembered seeing the impressive beaux-arts style of the buildings at the world's fair in Chicago. The Eason House has a prominent triangular roof, classical Greek columns, and plaster decorations. All of these design elements* were borrowed from older buildings. Over the next few years, Charles and Henry would design more houses with similar design elements.

> * design elements
> The different parts of an artistically arranged plan for a building.

33

Classical decoration.

Triangular roof shape.

Willis Eason House, 1895,
Pasadena, California.
Greene & Greene, Architects.

Ionic columns on the front porch.

Triangular roof shape.

Classical decoration.

Decorative windows.

Shaped columns
on the front porch.

There are three
porches.

Jacob Helmke House, 1896,
Pasadena, California.
Frederick Roehrig, Architect.

No classical decoration.

Triangular roof shape.

Decorative windows.

Frank Lloyd Wright House, 1889–1898, Oak Park, Illinois. Frank Lloyd Wright, Architect.

No columns on the porch.

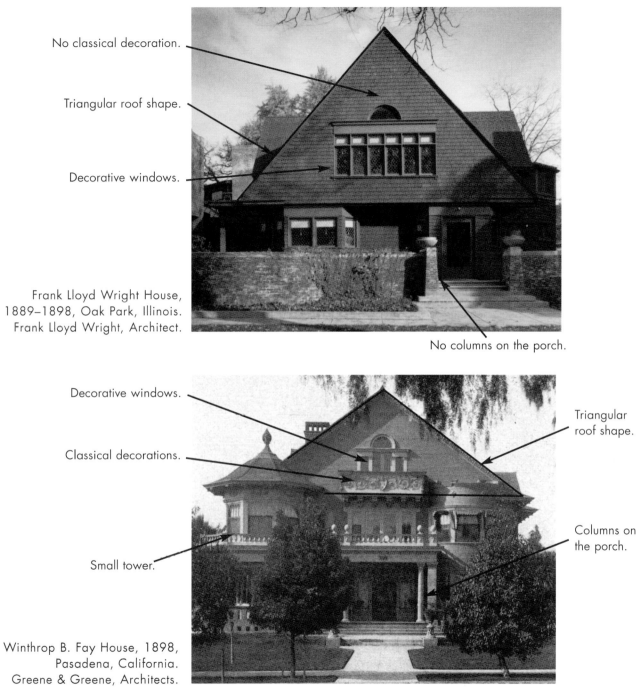

Decorative windows.

Classical decorations.

Small tower.

Triangular roof shape.

Columns on the porch.

Winthrop B. Fay House, 1898, Pasadena, California. Greene & Greene, Architects.

Draw a Symmetrical House

Symmetry is the exact matching in size, shape, and arrangement on either side of an imaginary line that is drawn through the center of an object. Here are photographs of two old houses. Which one is perfectly symmetrical? What makes the other house nonsymmetrical? Can you draw the nonsymmetrical house and then change it to a symmetrical house?

A New Century

By the 1900s, American homes had changed from the homes the Greene brothers grew up in. The new homes had many more modern conveniences, including electric lights, telephones, indoor toilets, bathtubs with running water, showers, running water in the kitchen sink, sewer pipes to remove waste from the house, improved central heating, and electric fans to circulate air. Electric outlets in the home provided power to run stoves, irons, kitchen appliances, vacuum cleaners, buzzers and doorbells, phonographs,* and in a few more years, radios. But there were still no refrigerators. Modern kitchens were equipped with a cool cupboard,** which was open to the outside air, and an icebox.***

*   An old-style record player.

**   A kitchen cupboard with an opening to the outside. Cold air enters the cupboard through the vent and keeps food cool.

***A large box with insulation kept cold with large blocks of ice.

This old postcard shows a dirigible balloon, an early airship, carrying ten passengers in a small basket-like structure underneath the balloon. The dirigible is flying over Pasadena's orange groves.

39

A poster for Women's Suffrage—women's right to vote.

Even with these modern conveniences, some household chores still took a lot of time. For example, doing the family's washing and ironing took an entire week. Still, new conveniences at home gave women more free time. Many more women were taking jobs outside the home. The Women's Suffrage movement was gaining strength.

If they could afford it, families could buy one of the first new cars. They were called horseless carriages or automobiles. People were amazed by Halley's Comet, the first motion pictures (movies), the first airplane flight, the newly formed FBI, the Statue of Liberty, and the discovery of antiseptics to fight germs. With the advent of steel-reinforced buildings, skyscrapers grew taller and taller. Visitors to Pasadena had the opportunity to take a ride in America's first passenger dirigible.

Children were enjoying new treats—chewing gum, dry cereal, and Coca Cola. They were reading *The Wizard of Oz* and picture books with color illustrations. They could join the Boy Scouts and the Girls Scouts, organizations created just for them. And best of all they were given comfortable clothes to wear while they played with teddy bears, Brownie cameras, roller skates, and Crayola crayons.

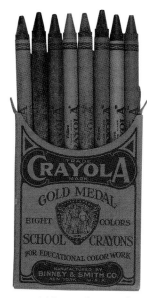

An old box of Crayola crayons.

This is the cover of an old coloring book.

John Muir spoke about preserving nature and President Teddy Roosevelt created a system of national parks. Everyone loved to work crossword puzzles.

In Pasadena the first Rose Bowl Game was played in 1902; a new observatory was built on Mount Wilson in 1905; and the Greene brothers were designing homes that would make them world famous.

11404.   Gamble Residence, Pasadena, Cal.

One of Charles and Henry's famous houses.

This horseless carriage needs two horses to pull it out of the water. Do you think people thought that early automobiles could travel through deep water the same as horses do?

Love and Marriage

The first years of the twentieth century were happy times for the Greene family. Both Charles and Henry fell in love, married, and started families of their own. Henry married Emeline Dart in Illinois, her home state. Charles married Alice White in Pasadena. Henry and Emeline honeymooned in the Midwest and then returned to Pasadena. Henry ran the office while Charles and Alice took a steamship to England for a long honeymoon. Alice had grown up in England and she must have wanted to show Charles her childhood home.

Charles enjoyed the charming English country houses and their flower gardens. The houses had a very natural look. They were built with wooden timbers in their natural color, rough hand-split shingles, called shakes, bricks in the natural clay color, and cement, which was textured with sand or small pebbles. These English houses were representative of the Arts & Crafts movement.

Emeline and Henry.

Hand-split wooden shakes were used in the construction of Arts & Crafts houses.

An English country house in the Arts & Crafts style.

The Arts & Crafts Movement

The Arts & Crafts movement was based on a philosophy of handwork and creative expression. It was promoted by a group of craftsmen, artists, designers, and architects. The movement began in England and then spread to the United States; it started around 1890 and ended around 1929. It attracted many followers who lived simpler quiet lifestyles in homes that reflected the popular Arts & Crafts style.

The Arts & Crafts movement was a reaction against industrialization, or the shift from making goods, chairs for example, by hand at home to making them with power machines in factories. In the late 1800s, industrialization was responsible for the movement of huge numbers of Americans from farms and small towns to cities.

Thread for cross-stitched handwork matched colors found in nature.

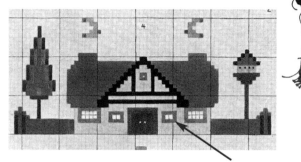

Women cross-stitched pictures of Arts & Crafts houses in their handwork. Does this house look like the English house on the opposite page?

Most new city residents earned enough money to live comfortably. But they weren't as happy as they had hoped to be. Cities were crowded and dirty. Life was hectic and more complicated. City dwellers missed the slower pace of life in the countryside. They couldn't go back to the past, but they could put some of the simplicity of the old days back into their lives. They could live in homes where there was peace and solitude, and where values from the past, such as the love of beautiful objects skillfully created by hand, were honored. This kind of thinking made the Arts & Crafts movement very popular.

This rocking chair, manufactured by well-known craftsman Gustav Stickley, was often found in Arts & Crafts homes.

Followers of the Arts & Crafts movement disliked homes cluttered* both inside and out with Victorian decorations. Arts & Crafts houses were built with natural, unpainted materials: wood, stone, and brick. Rooms were painted in soft green and gold colors accented with the natural color of wood cabinets and doors. They were sparsely** filled with only a few well-placed objects—handmade furniture, embroidered cloth, pottery, baskets, rugs, art metal, and lamps. It was soothing and peaceful inside an Arts & Crafts home.

* Too many objects
  in one room.

** Very few objects in
  one room.

A shell lamp by Arts & Crafts designer Louis Comfort Tiffany.

Oakholm

Henry and son.

Alice and son.

Henry and Emeline rented a cottage next to Henry's parents' house. They lived there until their first child was born; then they moved to a larger rented house in Los Angeles. Emeline's mother, Charlotte Whitridge, came to live with them because Emeline had poor health. Grandma Whitridge helped take care of the children.

A son was born to Charles and Alice and they needed a house for their family, too. Charles was eager to experiment with new design ideas. He had been reading about Japanese architecture and the growing Arts & Crafts movement in the eastern United States. It was lucky for them that Alice had enough money from her family to build a house.

Charles and Alice bought a piece of land on the banks of the Arroyo Seco. At that time, the Arroyo Seco was untouched by development. It was filled with wildlife—foxes, rabbits, coyotes, skunks, snakes, and birds—and with oak trees, sycamore trees, bay laurel trees, and native wildflowers.

This is Oakholm, Charles and Alice's house. The rock wall in front of the house is shown close-up on the next page.

Charles and Alice called their house "Oakholm" because it was built under the spreading branches of a gigantic old oak tree. Charles used natural materials to build the house. He used unpainted wood shingles, natural colored clay bricks, and smooth gray stones from the Arroyo Seco. The wall in front of the house is an excellent example of Arts & Crafts design. It used materials in their natural state and it was made by hand with the finest craftsmanship. When the wall was finished, it was more than a wall; it was a work of art.

Charles handpicked each stone. To the mix of stones of various sizes and shapes he added Pasadena's "clinker bricks." Clinker bricks were clay bricks that had been placed too close to the heat when they were fired in the oven or kiln. The heat melted the bricks into weird distorted shapes. Charles

loved them. They had shapes that might have been found in nature, like the twisted branches of an ancient Arroyo oak tree or the outcropping of rocks in the nearby mountains. The dark color of the clinker bricks contrasted perfectly with the soft gray stones. The wall didn't look man-made and brand new. It looked as though it grew naturally from the banks of the Arroyo Seco. It also looked like a magnificent piece of art or sculpture.

Oakholm was small, the perfect size for a young family. It had a large bathroom and modern kitchen. It had hiding places and hidden corners where children could play. As the Greene family grew in size so did the house. Charles stacked rooms for children one on top of the other, giving the top of the house a tower shape.

This is part of the wall that Charles Greene built in front of his house, Oakholm. He handpicked and placed every stone and clinker brick.

Clinker bricks.

47

Build a Model Stone Wall

Materials

 An assortment of small stones, which may be gathered in the yard or purchased from a nursery or landscape supply company

 One batch of Baker's Clay

 One square of sturdy cardboard

A close-up look at the Oakholm wall.

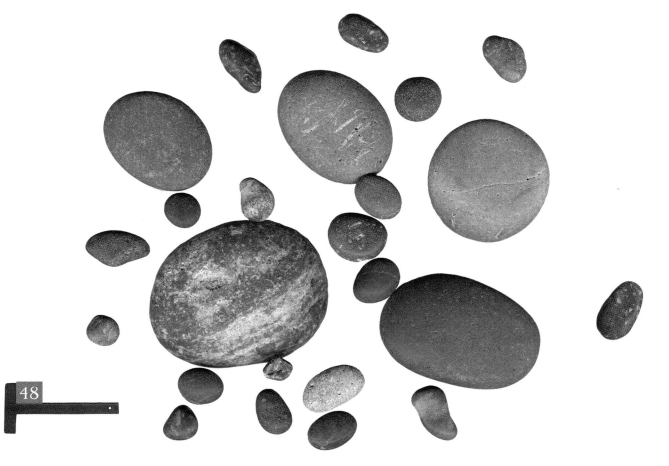

The cardboard will be the base of your wall. Place a small handful of Baker's Clay on the cardboard and begin building a stone wall. Add a layer of rocks and press them into the Baker's Clay. Then add another layer of clay. Smooth it down and press it onto the rocks. Continue adding layers of rock and clay until your wall is four or five layers high. Prop up the wall with a box until the Baker's Clay dries and feels hard to the touch.

Baker's Clay

4 cups unsifted all-purpose flour

1 cup salt

1 ½ cups water

Measure flour and salt and stir together in a large bowl. Add water slowly and then mix with your hands until dough is even in texture. If the dough is too hard to handle, add water, ¼ cup at a time, until the dough is not sticky and is easy to work with your hands. Knead the dough on a wooden surface for 4 to 6 minutes. The dough should be shaped immediately because it will dry out in about 4 hours.

The bricks were made with Spicy Dark Dough, page 80.

49

Influence from Japan

At the same time that many wealthy New Englanders became interested in the simple life of the Arts & Crafts movement, they also developed an interest in Japan.

Japan had been closed to contact with the outside world for almost two hundred years. Their government wanted to protect the Japanese people from exposure to what they called "outside barbarians." This meant that no ships from other nations could sail into a Japanese harbor or set foot on Japanese land.

This changed when a daring American naval officer, Admiral Matthew Perry, sailed his ship into Tokyo Bay and convinced the Japanese to sign a trade treaty with the United States. Many American shipping companies were headquartered in Boston. Soon trade ships with captains and crews from Boston began to visit Japan. They returned with stories about Japanese life and beautiful objects of Japanese art. The wealthy people of Boston took an interest in Japan.

In the early 1880s, Edward Morse traveled around Japan observing Japanese life and collecting pottery for two Boston museums. Morse also became interested in Japanese houses. A simple, traditional Japanese house filled with few objects was very appealing when compared with the ornate overdecorated Victorian homes back in Boston. When Morse returned to Boston, he turned his observations into a book called *Japanese Homes and Their Surroundings*. This book was very popular, and soon important American architects were using elements of Japanese style in their buildings.

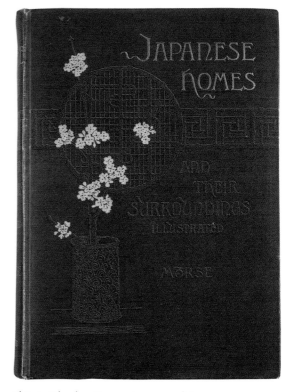

This is Charles Greene's copy of *Japanese Homes and Their Surroundings*.

This miniature Japanese robe was collected by the Gamble Family.

50

Japanese Homes and Their Surroundings was published while the Greene brothers were attending the Manual Training School in St. Louis. Charles and Henry were also exposed to Japanese art and its influence on American architecture while they lived in Boston. In later years, Charles owned his own copy of *Japanese Homes and Their Surroundings.* In 1904, Charles traveled to St. Louis to see the Japanese and Chinese exhibits at a large world's fair called the Louisiana Purchase Exhibition.

This is Greene & Greene's Longley House. It was built in 1897. Can you see that the roofs are similar in shape to the Japanese building?

This is an outdoor lantern at Greene & Greene's Gamble House. Can you see that the shape is similar to the Japanese lantern?

This is a Japanese building.

Make a Scrapbook

Set up your supplies on a clean table where you can work. Use the white paper to make the scrapbook pages. Fold the paper, one piece at a time, in half by bringing the long sides together. The paper will now be 5½ x 14 inches. Crease each fold with the flat side of your fingernail. Fold the colored paper in the same way to make a cover.

Fold each piece of paper in half again. The paper will now be 5½ x 7 inches. Flatten the fold with the flat side of your fingernail.

With the inside of the fold facing up, punch a hole at the top and the bottom of each piece of paper. It is easy to punch all of the holes in exactly the same place, if you slide the paper into the paper punch until it is stopped by the metal and then punch the paper.

Place the colored paper on the table with the inside of the fold facing up. Assemble the book: Place the pages, one at a time, inside the cover. Each sheet of paper has a folded side and an open side. Alternate the folded side to the top and bottom of the book. Thread the ribbon through the holes and tie in a bow. Decorate the cover with colorful origami paper.

Materials

8 pieces of white paper (11 x 17) and
1 sheet of colorful paper (11 x 17)
cut to 11 x 14

Ruler

Pencil

Single hole punch

36 inches of very thin ribbon

Package of colorful printed
origami paper

*Paper may be purchased at Kinkos
and cut to size (by an adult)
on the store's self-serve
paper cutter.*

Light Hall

Light Hall's two-story entrance.

Clients who came to the Greenes' office wanted traditional houses. Many people weren't ready for the new ideas of the Arts & Crafts movement and Japanese design. They liked the impressive house the Greenes designed for George Barker. The Barker House was called Light Hall, because the Barkers owned a local electricity plant. And "light hall" it was! The Greenes designed an impressive two-story entrance hall that was painted bright white and wired with a large number of electric lights. Light Hall was an excellent commission, but the Greenes must have wanted to try out some of the ideas that Charles was experimenting with in his new home.

1022:—Palatial Home, Pasadena, Cal.

A decorative window.

Triangle shaped roof.

Classical columns.

A postcard showing the beaux-arts Barker House. This house is also known as Light Hall.

The Culbertson House

An English Arts & Crafts house. Like the Culbertson House, it is made from wooden shingles and plaster.

Good fortune sent Charles and Henry the perfect clients: James and Nora Culbertson. The Culbertsons had a lovely English-style Arts & Crafts home in Kenilworth, an exclusive suburb north of Chicago. Chicago winters were long and cold, and the Culbertsons wished to build a similar home in Pasadena where the winter weather was warm and pleasant. They were wealthy and offered Charles and Henry an excellent opportunity to design a romantic Arts & Crafts house.

Pieces of wood, called half timber, make a simple design on the side of this house.

The Culbertson roof extends beyond the walls.

There are no beaux-arts columns or decorations.

The Culbertson House has half-timber designs.

This is the house Charles and Henry designed for James Culbertson in 1902. It looks more like the English house than the Barker House, which was designed by the Greenes in the same year.

Design a Motto

Mottos are words to live by. Here is a drawing of a motto that Charles made to use as a pattern for a wood carving in the Culbertson House. You can see how clever he was to draw the letters as objects. Create your own drawing using the motto on the next page. (Several mottos are available as downloads at www.greeneandgreeneforkids.com.)

Begin by drawing the words on the paper in pencil. Use the tracing paper to plan your designs for the first letters of each word. Draw the designs on the paper, and color them if you like.

Materials

Good quality white drawing paper

A soft drawing pencil

Tracing paper

Colored pencils

The letter "T" is also a flowerpot.

The letter "B" is a pitcher.

The letter "T" is a table and the letter "h" is a chair.

A chicken is standing on the letter "I."

Two fish make the letter "O."

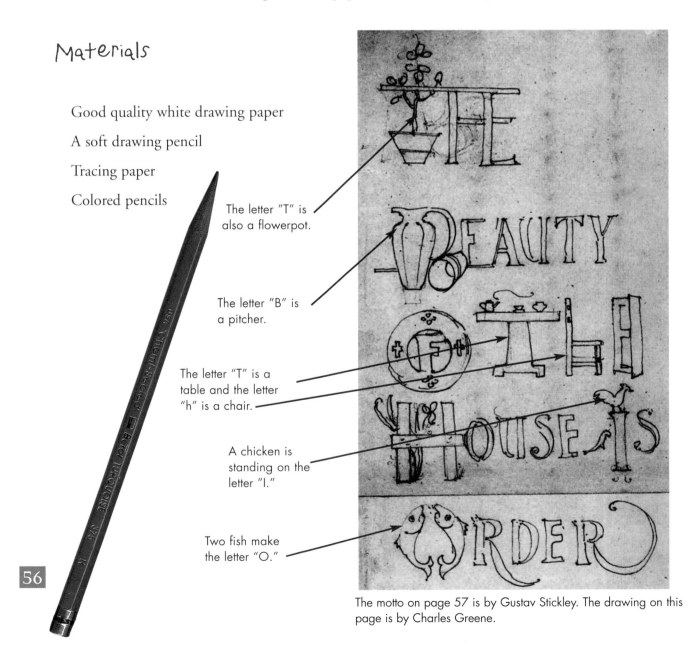

The motto on page 57 is by Gustav Stickley. The drawing on this page is by Charles Greene.

56

Be
the Best
You
Can Be

Charles hand carved wooden panels for the Culbertson House, adding his art and craft to the architectural design. Some of the carvings had special sayings or mottos. The mottos were placed around the house where they would greet visitors and remind them of the proper mood for entering the Culbertson House. The Culbertsons were very happy with their new Arts & Crafts home.

This is a panel carved by Charles along with some of the chisels Charles used for wood carving.

The Bungalow

This is a drawing of a one-story bungalow from the Bengal region of India.

This is a picture of a tall Victorian-style house.

American families were beginning to grow tired of living in dark row houses and cramped apartments. By 1900, they wanted a home of their own, and city jobs earned them enough extra money to pay for one. The bungalow style of house was the perfect model for a reasonably priced home. It arrived in America exactly when the American Arts & Crafts movement was gaining strength.

The bungalow traces its beginning to the Bengal region of India where long ago it was a typical kind of country home. It is a small, simple one-story building with a porch running along all four sides. A bungalow is not connected to other homes. It stands alone and is surrounded by a private yard. Because all of the rooms in these early bungalows opened onto a porch, fresh air could circulate throughout the house. Simplicity of design, fresh air, and privacy were features of the earliest bungalows.

Europeans who lived in India added their own modern conveniences to the bungalow, but the idea behind it remained the same. A bungalow represented a return to a simpler way of life. It was a private place to reflect and be at peace with the world and with one's self. The bungalow was a perfect fit with the principles of the American Arts & Crafts movement. Compared to tall Victorian houses, bungalows are low and close to the ground. In a bungalow, most of the rooms are on the ground floor, although some larger bungalows have a smaller second floor. A typical one-story bungalow has a central living room with bedrooms, a bathroom, and a kitchen.

Most American bungalows built in the early 1900s were small and they could be purchased for a very reasonable sum of money. Skilled architects designed many of them. In fact, this was one of the only times in the history of American architecture when a family with an average income could afford to buy a home designed by a very good architect.

This is an old advertisement for a modern Los Angeles bungalow.

Architects designed bungalows inside and out. They furnished them with built-in cabinets, bookshelves, benches, and window seats. It was a complete approach to simple family living—a perfect place to live. If a family could not afford to hire an architect to design their bungalow, it was possible to choose a bungalow from a catalog and then purchase the pre-made pieces needed to build it.

Bungalows had all of the very newest modern appliances—electric stoves, hot running water, vacuum cleaners, and electric irons. This allowed American homemakers more freedom by saving them many hours of housework. With modern conveniences, less time was spent in the kitchen. The simple design made bungalows and Arts & Crafts furniture easier to clean. There was no more dusting Victorian knickknacks or washing and ironing clothes with miles of fancy Victorian lace trimmings.

This is an early toaster.

This old drawing, called a cross-section, shows the living room of a bungalow, above, and a modern coal-fired furnace, below. Would this furnace be considered modern today?

Bungalow-style houses had spread from India to England by the time Charles and Henry moved to Pasadena in 1893. By 1900, Americans were bungalow crazy. Bungalows or small single-family houses with a garden and a yard sprouted up wherever families had money to pay for them. Southern California was the bungalow's perfect home. It had a warm, sunny climate, land available for a cheap price, a growing population, and eastern families that could afford to live in a warmer and healthier place. Even though bungalows were built all over the United States, the words "California" and "bungalow" are usually said together. The bungalow craze joined with the popular Arts & Crafts movement to create the California craftsman bungalow.

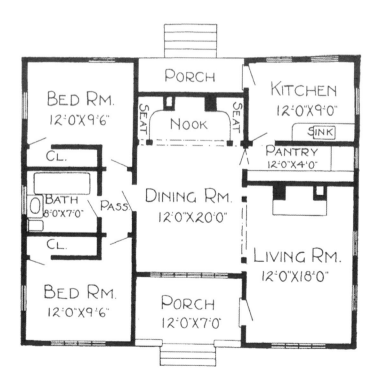

This is a typical bungalow floor plan. Can you see why it is not the floor plan for the bungalow in the picture above?

Neighborhood Bungalows

Here are pictures of four houses. Are all of them bungalows? Why? Can you find four bungalows in your neighborhood?

Characteristics of a Bungalow

1. A bungalow is not connected to other homes.

2. A bungalow is surrounded by a private yard.

3. Bungalows are low and close to the ground.

4. Most of the rooms in a bungalow are on the ground floor.

5. Some larger bungalows have a smaller second floor.

6. Bungalows have a porch on the front side of the house.

7. Even though some bungalows have a second story, the long low lines of the roof make them look low and close to the ground.

In this picture, Henry is at the drawing board, hard at work.

By 1902, Charles and Henry were designing Arts & Crafts bungalows, called "craftsman bungalows" for short. Houses built in 1903 for Mary Darling, and 1904 for Edgar Camp, are examples of Charles and Henry's craftsman bungalows.

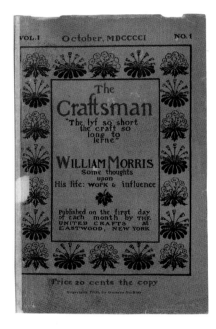

An old picture of the Camp House in Sierra Madre, California.

Gustav Stickley's magazine, *The Craftsman*, gave the Greenes information on the Arts & Crafts movement in other parts of the country and the world. This was helpful and important knowledge in days before travel to other states and countries was commonplace.

To the right is a picture of the Darling House in Claremont, California. This is the way the house looks today.

Greene & Greene bungalows were dark. The sun is bright and hot in Southern California. Before air-conditioning, houses were very warm in the summer. Charles and Henry's craftsman bungalows were stained in dark colors to give relief from the bright California sun. The roof projected beyond the walls of the house to shade the windows from the hot sun, but it also made the house dark inside.

These windows have a small roof over them to protect the house from the strong glare of the sun.

The walls are covered with hand-cut wooden shakes in a natural wood color.

The roof of the Darling House has only one triangular shape. The long sides of the triangle are not as steep as they were in the Greenes' beaux-arts-style houses.

When the house was built, this was an open porch over the front door. You can see what it might have looked like in the drawing on page 70.

Charles is reading an architectural drawing.

By 1906, Charles and Henry were very successful. Color-tinted postcards with pictures of their houses were being sent as souvenirs of a visit to Pasadena. They had challenging, creative work and wealthy clients who were willing to spend a lot of money. One of them was the widow of a former president of the United States—James A. Garfield.

A Residence on Oak Knoll, Pasadena, Cal.

11404. Gamble Residence, Pasadena, Cal.

2658 — Southern California Winter Home of Mrs. Jas A. Garfield at Pasadena.

Mix Arts & Crafts Colors

The primary colors are red, yellow, and blue. The secondary colors are orange, green, and violet (purple). The secondary colors are made by mixing two of the primary colors together.

Red + Yellow = Orange • Yellow + Blue = Green • Blue + Red = Violet

When we look at this color wheel we see how the colors blend together to form a circle of continuous colors. The colors in the color wheel are bright. Arts & Crafts artists loved color, but they did not use the bright primary colors very often. They did not use them on the walls of their homes or in the colors of their furniture or decorations. Instead they used shades and tints of the bright colors on the color wheel. When we add black to a color the result is called a *shade.* When we add white to a color the result is called a *tint.* The Arts & Crafts artists often used shades and tints of the bright colors in their work because they provided a softer background.

The brilliant colors in a flower garden on a bright sunny day are like the colors on the color wheel. The soft colors found in nature on a misty gray day are like the shades and tints of colors used by the Arts & Crafts artists.

This color wheel was painted by a child. The red and blue colors are lighter than they should be. The wheel also shows the colors made by mixing the primary and secondary colors with their neighbors.

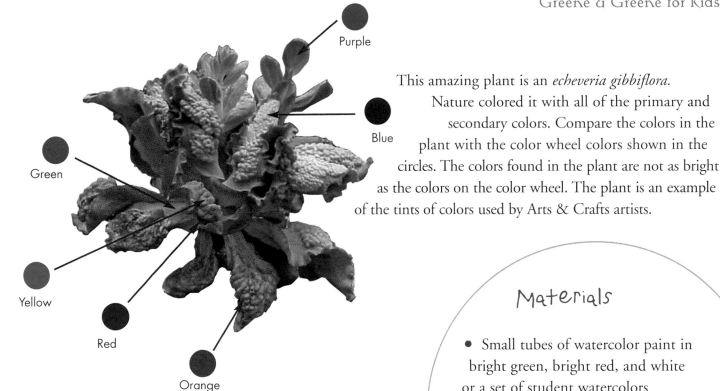

Purple

Blue

Green

Yellow

Red

Orange

This amazing plant is an *echeveria gibbiflora*. Nature colored it with all of the primary and secondary colors. Compare the colors in the plant with the color wheel colors shown in the circles. The colors found in the plant are not as bright as the colors on the color wheel. The plant is an example of the tints of colors used by Arts & Crafts artists.

Materials

- Small tubes of watercolor paint in bright green, bright red, and white or a set of student watercolors

- Watercolor brush of medium quality

- Sheet of watercolor paper

- Glass of clean water

- Paint-mixing dish

How to mix Complementary Colors

Red and green are complementary colors. Complementary colors are opposite each other on the color wheel. When complementary colors are mixed together in small amounts they make the muted shades found in the *echeveria gibbiflora*. These muted shades that are found in nature were used by the Greene brothers.

Squeeze small amounts of each color onto the paint-mixing dish. Wet the brush with water and mix a small amount of red with an equal amount of green. Wash the brush in the water and add a small amount of white. Wash the brush again, and then continue adding small amounts of white until the color approximates the swatch shown on the far right below.

69

The Color Drawing Mystery

Charles Greene's design for a house was published in an English magazine. The black-and-white drawing below is an illustration from the magazine. The drawing was probably made with colored watercolors. The original drawing has disappeared. All that remains is this version made from a copy of the old magazine. It is black and white because the drawing was not printed in color.

You can download the drawing at www.greeneandgreeneforkids.com. Print two copies. Use watercolor pens or a computer drawing program to color the picture the way you think Charles would have colored it. Then color another copy of the picture the way you would like to color it.

Do you think the drawing below is of the Darling House? How many similarities do you see between the photograph and the drawing?

An example of the drawing in color.

The Craftsmen

Charles and Henry Greene did not actually build the houses they designed. Talented contractors and their skilled workmen built the finely crafted Greene & Greene homes. Without their careful attention to detail and superior craftsmanship, the Greenes would not have been able to create their magnificent homes.

Two brothers, John and Peter Hall, built many of the Greenes' best-known houses. The Halls were very close in age to the Greenes, and, like the Greenes, they worked together as a team. John was a skilled cabinet-maker and he built furniture and crafted fine wood-work for the Greenes. Peter supervised the framing and details of the houses.

The Halls and the Greenes' other contractors were helped by fine craftsmen who made tiles for fireplaces, art glass for windows, and art metal for hanging lamps. The picture shows a group of craftsmen working at the Irwin House in 1906.

John Hall.

Peter Hall.

73

Architectural Drawings

When the Greenes had ideas about the design of a house, they drew sketches to show the client what the house would look like. Contractors and craftsmen also needed drawings from the Greenes so they could build their houses exactly the way the Greenes wanted them built. Houses have three dimensions—length, height, and depth—and the drawing had only length and height. How did the contractors work from these drawings?

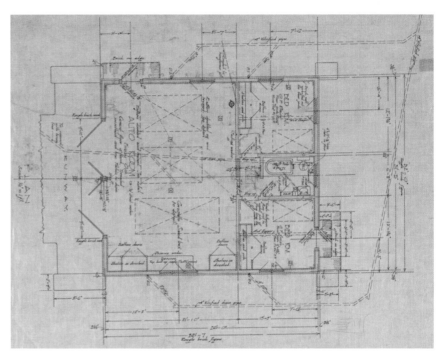

This is the floor plan for the Gamble House garage. It is the same view as the top view of the Ivory Badger soap carving.

This is the front elevation of the Gamble House garage. It is the same view as the front view of the Ivory Badger soap carving.

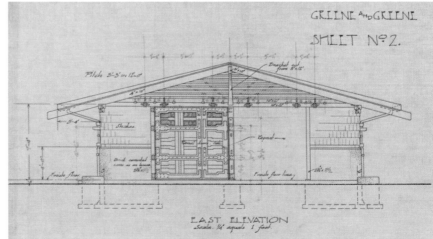

74

The office of Architects Greene & Greene had several men and one woman who drew or drafted the drawings for the houses. A set of drawings for a house is sometimes called the "plans." The floor plan is the most informative. This plan is a bird's-eye view of the floor of the house and it gives the contractor a lot of important information. The contractor also needs information about the three-dimensional aspects of the house. The drawings, called elevations, provide this information.

If you carve the Ivory Badger on page 6, you will have a better understanding of how a contractor uses a set of two-dimensional plans to build a three-dimensional house.

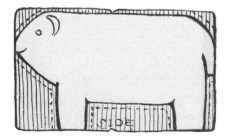

BACK

This is a side (south) elevation of the Gamble House garage. It is the same view as the back view of the Ivory Badger soap carving.

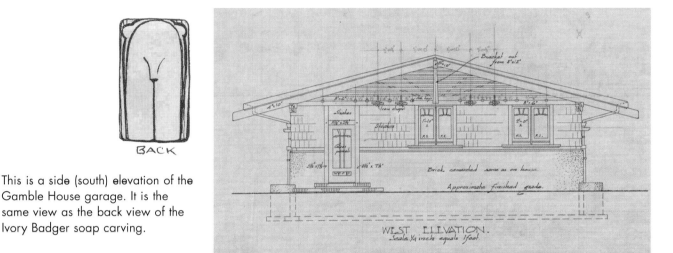

WEST ELEVATION.
Scale ¼ inch equals 1 foot.

SIDE

This is a side (south) elevation of the Gamble House garage. It is the same view as the side view of the Ivory Badger soap carving.

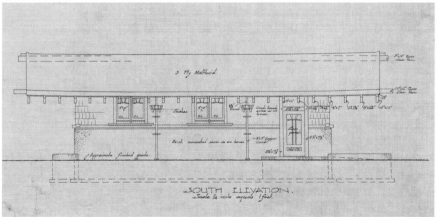

SOUTH ELEVATION.
Scale ¼ inch equals 1 foot.

Ultimate Bungalows

An ultimate bungalow is a very large and formal house that was designed for very rich clients. These houses have many features of the smaller bungalows, but are really too big to be called bungalows. In recent years they have been nicknamed "ultimate bungalows" because these houses are thought to be of the finest design and quality of construction. The Blacker House is the ultimate bungalow shown on these pages.

Ultimate bungalows needed as many as six full-time servants to take care of them! The servants usually lived in very small bedrooms tucked away into a far corner of the house. They had their own small bathroom, eating area, and private stairway. They wore special uniforms while they worked.

At the front of the house there was a large entrance hall with a grand staircase.

Downstairs there was a large living room. There was also a guest bedroom with a private bathroom. This was later turned into a library.

Near the kitchen was a large dining room with a fireplace.

There were covered porches off some bedrooms that were used (before air-conditioning) for sleeping outside on hot nights.

Below the house was a basement with a large laundry room.

Upstairs there were four large family bedrooms with fireplaces and private bathrooms. There were also additional bedrooms for servants.

There were several large outdoor porches.

The cook.

The chauffeur sometimes did gardening.

The maid.

The yard was large and had a fishpond and flower gardens. There might also be a vegetable garden for the cook.

These are the rooms in a small craftsman bungalow.

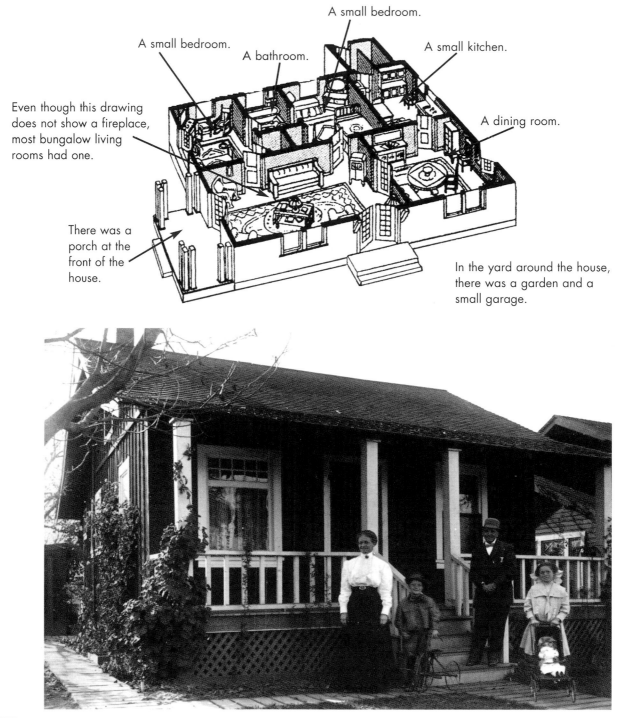

A small bedroom.

A small bedroom.

A bathroom.

A small kitchen.

Even though this drawing does not show a fireplace, most bungalow living rooms had one.

A dining room.

There was a porch at the front of the house.

In the yard around the house, there was a garden and a small garage.

It took two parents to take care of a craftsman bungalow.

The Bungalow Fireplace

The fireplace was the center of a bungalow home. It was where the family gathered to exchange news of the day and to warm themselves by the fire in cold weather. The space around the fireplace was pleasing to the eye and inviting to the soul. It was often the most attractive space in the room.

After 1911, the Greenes often used tiles made by a local Pasadena craftsman named Ernest Batchelder. Batchelder carved whimsical designs into the flat surface of the tile. He sculpted vines, trees, plants and animals, and European scenes with castles, boats, and sailboats. The tiles shown below were made by Ernest Batchelder.

Design an Arts & Crafts Tile

Spicy Dark Dough Ingredients

$\frac{1}{3}$ cup shortening

1 cup firmly packed brown sugar

1 (12 fluid ounce) bottle of molasses

$\frac{2}{3}$ cup water

6+ cups sifted flour

2 teaspoons baking soda

1 teaspoon salt

$\frac{1}{2}$ teaspoon cinnamon

$\frac{1}{4}$ teaspoon nutmeg

$\frac{1}{4}$ teaspoon ginger

To Make Spicy Dark Dough

You will need an adult to help you make this recipe.

Mix together the shortening, brown sugar, and molasses until completely blended. Add water. Note: The dough will appear to curdle at this point. The curdling will disappear when you add the flour.

Measure and sift the flour, salt, baking soda, and spices. Mix these ingredients into the dough. Add flour until you can work the dough without it sticking to your hands. Scrape dough from the bowl and store in an airtight container until ready to use. Unused dough may be kept in the refrigerator for up to a week.

Materials

Interesting objects found around the house

One recipe Spicy Dark Dough

3-inch square cookie cutter (optional)

Dull dinner table knife

A tool for lemons is an interesting object.

To Make the Arts & Crafts Tile

You will need an adult to help you make your tile.

Find a clean place where you can work. Gather together some interesting objects found in the kitchen or around the house. Some examples are shown below. Roll out one-fourth of the Dark Dough on a sheet of waxed paper to about three-fourths to 1-inch thick. The dough should be a uniform thickness. Cut several 3-inch squares using a cookie cutter or a paper pattern and a dull knife. Transfer each square to a clean piece of waxed paper.

You can use the found objects to press designs into the dough or you can mold shapes with your hands and press them onto the top of the tile. Use the designs shown on this page as patterns to follow or make up designs of your own. If you make up your own designs you may want to draw them on graph paper first. Don't cut too deep into your dough—you will need a solid surface of dough to support the finished tile.

When you have finished carving your designs, carefully move the tiles to a lightly greased baking sheet and bake in a 350º oven for 15 minutes. When the tiles have cooled, carefully remove them with a spatula.

A tool for serving honey can make patterns on your tile.

A sculpture tool from an art store is good for carving shapes.

A fork makes a useful tool.

The Gamble House

The Gamble House, built in 1908, is the ultimate "ultimate bungalow" designed by Charles and Henry Greene. It was built as an elegant winter home for a very wealthy family from Cincinnati—the Gambles of the Procter & Gamble Company. Don't you think that Procter & Gamble must have sold a lot of Ivory Soap to allow the Gamble family to build this amazing home?

Three generations of Gambles in their special Pasadena car. The smallest child in this photo remembered her trips to Pasadena:

"We'd ride in the train for days, bundled up in our warmest clothes. Crossing the desert we'd take off our heavy coats. Then suddenly, we were in California, and soon we pulled into the drive at Westmoreland Place. In Pasadena we could wear our light dresses and drive around town in Papa's car—his special Pasadena car. It felt like Paradise."

11409. West Morland Place, Pasadena, Cal.

The Gamble House was built on Westmoreland Place in 1907–9.

People with money often collect fine art, such as paintings and sculptures, and display their collections in their homes. For the Gamble family, their house was their art collection. The rooms and all of the furnishings were art created by Charles and Henry Greene.

The Gamble House living room is very large, so large that a visitor might feel uncomfortable sitting alone in such a large space. The Greenes created smaller, more comfortable spaces within the living room by adding two alcoves.* One was an inglenook** and one was a large bay window.*** The inglenook and the bay window are exactly opposite each other. They are open to the larger part of the room but heavy, low, wooden swooping shapes separate the alcoves as though a line has been drawn to visually separate them.

*   An alcove is a small space with three walls—like a closet without a door—within a larger room.

** An inglenook is an alcove with a fireplace.

*** A bay window is an alcove with windows on all three walls.

A built-in bench on one side of the inglenook. The Gamble House has a large inglenook. Most bungalows have small inglenooks.

The Gamble House living room. This photo is taken from the bay window alcove.

The inglenook is kind of dark. Inside are a fireplace, cabinets, and two built-in benches. It is a cozy space to sit at night and watch a fire. By contrast, the bay window alcove is a place to sit during the day. It is very bright. The person who sits in this alcove will want to look outside at the terrace, fishpond, yard, and beyond. Arts & Crafts architects often used the symbolism of the four natural elements—earth, air, water, and fire—to bring nature inside their houses. The inglenook in the Gamble House represents earth (with clay tiles) and fire (with the fireplace). The alcove in the Gamble House offers a view of air and water (with the fishpond).

The bay window alcove.

The inglenook alcove.

Heavy, low swooping shapes, called trusses, visually separate the alcoves from the room. These shapes remind us of Japanese designs.

A flower theme in the tiles of the fireplace is repeated in the glass of the cabinet doors. The hanging lanterns and larger light fixtures in the center of the room also repeat a similar design. This unity of themes, in this case the small flower design, is carried throughout the house.

The living room walls are covered with wood that has a warm, rich brown color and a smooth satiny finish. At the very top of the walls are scenes of birds and trees that were hand carved along the natural grain of the wood. The ceiling is painted a soft gray-green. The total effect was a soothing, peaceful living space for the Gamble family.

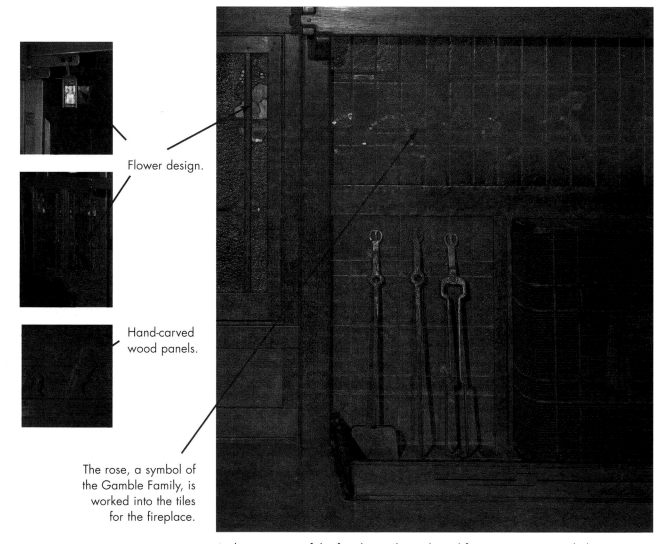

Flower design.

Hand-carved wood panels.

The rose, a symbol of the Gamble Family, is worked into the tiles for the fireplace.

A close-up view of the fireplace. The tools and fire screen were made by a craftsman metalworker.

Orange Grove Ave., Pasadena Cal.

This is a picture of a famous old oak tree that stood for many years in the middle of a road. A tree like this inspired Charles and Henry Greene to create the Gamble House doors.

California oak leaves.

The Gamble House front doors have the design of an oak tree in the colored glass.

Make a Miniature Stained Glass Window

Charles and Henry Greene used colored glass or "stained glass" windows in many of their homes. The window shown on the front cover of this book is an example of the Greenes' work in stained glass. With a package or two of tumbled glass pieces from the Judson Studios in Los Angeles, you can make your own miniature stained glass window. The Judson Studios have been making and repairing stained glass windows for over one hundred years.

This is a window from the Pratt House.

Small pieces of glass were used to make this flower design.

Materials

One 8 x 10 inch clear plastic box frame
from Aaron Brothers or Michaels Stores

Jar of Mod Podge glue

One or two packages of tumbled flat glass fragments from the Judson Studios.
These may be ordered from www.greeneandgreeneforkids.com
or purchased at the Gamble House Bookstore, Pasadena, California.

88

You need a clear plastic box frame. Clean the surface of the plastic with a damp cloth. Arrange the tumbled glass fragments on the plastic in a pleasing design. Carefully dot the back of each piece of glass with a small amount of Mod Podge. Set the glass on the top of the plastic box frame and let the glue dry overnight. Prop the box frame up against a window so you can view your design with light coming through it.

The glass shapes inspired a sailboat design in this miniature stained glass window.

Note: The tumbled glass fragments have smooth edges. This glass does not break easily. If it does break, you will need an adult to help you dispose of the broken glass. If you cannot easily obtain the tumbled glass pieces from Judson Studios, other kinds of glass may be used such as mosaic glass from an art supply store or fish tank glass. However, the glue may not work as well on these materials and they won't be as transparent as the Judson Studio glass.

Does the Gamble House Have Any Secrets?

The Gamble House has hidden cupboards, a hidden sink in an upstairs bedroom, hidden lights in the living room alcove, and a hidden panel in the front hall that hides the entrance to the kitchen and the servants' stairs.

Some visitors to the house say that Aunt Julia's ghost still haunts her upstairs bedroom. Aunt Julia was Mrs. Gamble's sister. She was very kindly and everyone liked her. Because she never got married, she lived with Mr. and Mrs. Gamble. After Mr. and Mrs. Gamble died, Aunt Julia lived on in the house until she died. Some nights when it is very quiet in the Gamble House, you can hear Aunt Julia's footsteps on the stairs.

Aunt Julia.

Write a story about a ghost living in an old house. If you like, you may use one of these paragraphs as the beginning for your story.

I thought I was all alone in the big old house. Then I heard a door slam upstairs. Footsteps were running down the hall. Mugs, the cat, heard it, too. He sat very still, watching to see who would come downstairs. But no one came . . .

Mugs the cat and I were alone by the fireplace one night. I was sick so I had stayed home when everyone else went out to dinner. I heard a door open upstairs and footsteps in the hall. I reached out for Mugs but he was gone. I watched white-faced as the sound of the footsteps came down the stairs and the front door opened and closed. Then I saw Mugs over in the corner. He looked like one of those cats you see at Halloween . . .

This is Aunt Julia's room in the Gamble House.

The Pratt House

Another house that the Greenes designed was for a successful businessman named Charles Pratt. He and his wife, Mary, lived in the eastern United States. They were fond of rustic architecture and owned a camp, the local word for a country house, in upstate New York.

The Pratts bought a large piece of land in the beautiful Ojai (o-high) Valley near Santa Paula, California, and hired Charles and Henry to design the new house. The Greenes must have been very pleased with the new commission. This was their first opportunity to build an ultimate bungalow in the countryside.

The Pratts' land was fourteen acres, or the size of two large city blocks. Charles and Henry hiked around the land and studied the views of the surrounding mountains. They finally picked a building site where the house would best blend in with nature.

A foundation of smooth river stones and clinker bricks made the house look as if it had grown up out of the valley. The walls were covered with hand-cut wood shingles. Several low roofs projecting over the walls of the house at different angles mirrored the shapes of the mountains in the background.

When the photographer visited the Pratt House, these kittens were sleeping on the porch.

In most Greene & Greene ultimate bungalows, visitors enter through a spacious hall with a large staircase leading to the upper floor. The Pratt House is quite different. There is no spacious hall. Visitors enter directly into the living room. The living room is warm and cozy—just like a cabin. There is a small dining room off to one side of the living room. Visitors might find the Pratt House to be rather small. But if they were invited to spend the night, they would change their minds. A door to the right of the living room fireplace opens onto a large hall with a large stairway and four big, comfortable bedrooms.

Charles and Henry skillfully created a small cabin atmosphere in a very large house by separating the living room, dining room, and kitchen from the hallway, staircase, and bedrooms.

Charles and Henry worked on the Pratt House for four years, during 1908 through 1911. Work ended when they thought every detail was perfect and when the Pratts were tired of living in a house under construction.

The Greenes made this fireplace asymmetrical.

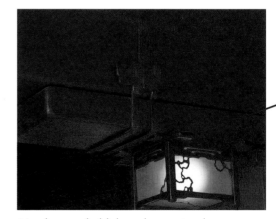
Metal straps hold these beams in place.

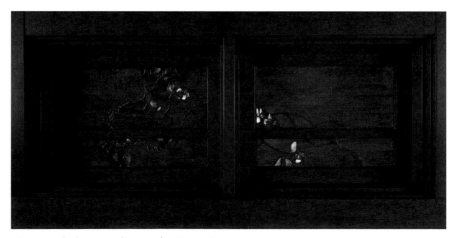
A stained glass window in the Pratt House.

Greene
& Greene
lantern.

Fireplace.

The door
is here.

Dinosaur.

Diagonal
pattern in
the floor.

The Pratt House living room.

95

This is the children's bedroom in the Pratt House. It has a fireplace and a sleeping porch.

The pantry is between the dining room and the kitchen.

The bathroom.

The Magic of Photography

The view from the Pratt House living room. The photographer has made it look like a magical garden.

Dinosaur.

Because of photography, anyone can look at the houses designed by Charles and Henry Greene without actually visiting them in person. Old photographs also show us exactly what the Greenes' houses looked like when they were first built.

The viewfinder is in the back of the camera.

This old camera does not take digital pictures. It uses film and it works as well today as it did when it was new. In fact, it was used to take many of the pictures in this book.

The film is inside the camera.

The shutter is in here.

A Brief History of Photography

Photographs are made when light passes through the lens of a camera and is captured on film. Photography as we know it was invented in France in the 1830s. The earliest photographs, called daguerreotypes, were made on thin sheets of glass. George Eastman invented flexible film (the kind we use in our cameras) in the United States in 1884. The first film was black and white. A color film was developed a few years later.

In 1886, Eastman invented the box camera. By 1900, one of Eastman's box cameras, called the Brownie, was so inexpensive that many people could afford to own one.

Personal cameras were one of the latest crazes when Charles and Henry opened their architecture office in Pasadena. Henry was interested in photography when he lived in Boston. In fact, some of his earliest photographs still exist today. Perhaps Henry's interest in photography is the reason there are so many photographs of Greene & Greene houses when they were first built.

Camera Terminology

SHUTTER—the spiral mechanism that opens when a button is pressed, allowing light to reach the film in the camera

VIEWFINDER—the little window in a camera that allows you to see what will be in your picture

EXPOSURE—the length of time the film is exposed to light

DAGUERREOTYPE—an early photographic print made on glass

FILM OR NEGATIVE—a flexible material that captures the negative image of light

PRINT—a positive paper image made from negative film

KODAK—this brand name comes from the sound made by the clicking of early cameras' shutters

Take Pictures of the Houses in Your Neighborhood

Camera loaded with color snapshot film
(a disposable camera will work, too)
Notebook and Pencil

Take photographs of twelve houses in your neighborhood at about 5 PM in the summer and 3 PM in the winter. The light is softer in the early morning and late afternoon and you will get better results.

You cannot walk onto your neighbor's property to take a picture without permission, so take your photographs from the sidewalk. Dark houses are harder to photograph so choose houses that are light in color. Stand opposite of the middle of the house and hold the camera as straight as you can. Look through the camera's viewfinder and make sure that you can see all of the house, including the roof and either side. When you have the picture lined up, snap the shutter. Use the notebook to write down the address of the house and the time of day you took the photograph. When you have taken all of the shots on the roll of film, have it processed and look over your work. Can you see anything you would have done differently? Can you recognize the architectural style of any of the houses? Are any of the houses bungalows?

Questions to Ask before You Take the Pictures

What is the most interesting thing in the photograph?

What is the exact time of day?

Is the sun behind you, in front of you, or is it a cloudy day?

Are there any unwanted objects in the pictures, such as trashcans, wires, cars, etc.?

Is a tree blocking the view of the house? If so, would you be better off taking the picture from an angle?

This house has a beautiful tree in the front. The tree and the triangular shape of the roof make this an interesting picture.

This house is painted bright blue. It makes an interesting picture because the house has columns and beaux-arts decorations. These decorations are usually found on larger houses.

More Changes

In 1913, the federal government passed a law requiring all citizens to pay income tax. After the taxes were paid, there was not as much money to build large, expensive houses. Work in Charles and Henry's office slowed down.

The popularity of craftsman bungalow architecture was ending. New clients were interested in English-style architecture. The Greenes designed a large English-style house in San Diego for Mary Kew. This house looked somewhat like the Greenes' first Arts & Crafts house, the James Culbertson House.

The James Culbertson House has roof shapes called gables.

Both houses have two chimneys.

Look carefully at these houses. How many other similarities can you see?

The Kew House has similar roof shapes called gables.

The Kew House has a porch that is similar to that of the Culbertson House.

101

Did Greene & Greene Houses Have a Place to Play?

Host a Tea Party

You Will Need:

Paper and colored markers to make invitations

Stickers, glue, glitter (optional)

Tray

Teapot and teacups

Paper napkins

Water

2 chamomile (or other herb) tea bags and hot water

Small pitcher of milk

Honey

Plate of cookies or other treats

In this picture, Henry Greene's children are having a tea party. Tea parties were a common social pastime when Charles and Henry Greene were working as architects.

Make an invitation for each tea party guest. Write them out by hand and then decorate them with colored markers. You can also decorate them with stickers or glitter if you want. Or you can print out your invitations on the computer. Before the tea party, gather together the tray, teapot and cups, napkins, tea bags, milk, and honey. Make a plate of treats you want to serve. These could be toast with jam, crackers, small sandwiches, cookies, or other treats you enjoy.

Cover a table with a cloth and set out the dishes and napkins. Have an adult make the tea. When the tea cools, carry it to the table on the tray. Serve your guests before you serve yourself. Have fun and remember to clean up after the party.

Make a Private Hideaway

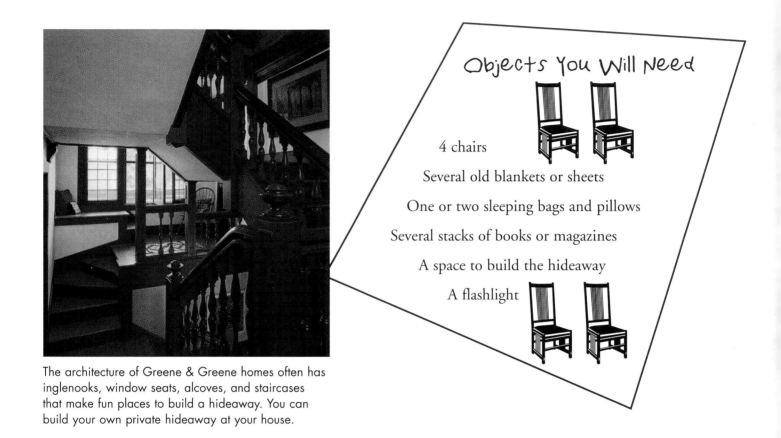

The architecture of Greene & Greene homes often has inglenooks, window seats, alcoves, and staircases that make fun places to build a hideaway. You can build your own private hideaway at your house.

Objects You Will Need

4 chairs

Several old blankets or sheets

One or two sleeping bags and pillows

Several stacks of books or magazines

A space to build the hideaway

A flashlight

Ask an adult to suggest an out-of-the-way place to build your hideaway. Gather all of the materials for your hideaway together in that place. Place the chairs at the four points of a square with their backs facing the inside of the square. Cover the floor with sleeping bags and pillows. Cover the chairs with blankets and hold the blankets in place with a stack of books or magazines placed on the seat of each chair. You may want to add more blankets or sheets to make the hideaway completely enclosed. Have fun!

Enter through
a tunnel.

Create a Small Water Garden

Materials

A round plastic bowl or tub container at least
  35 inches in diameter and 18 inches deep

3 or 4 medium-sized rocks about 8 inches in diameter

Small bag of potting soil

Water plants (Some plants may be found at local nurseries or you can order plants from the
children's garden from Van Ness Water Gardens at www.vannesswatergardens.com)

Water neutralizing solution (to remove chloramines and ammonia from tap water) from the fish store

Goldfish, mosquito fish, or water snails if you like

Goldfish can live in
the water garden.

You will need an adult to help you get the plastic container and other items for your water garden. You can
probably find rocks in the backyard or at a local building supply store.

Scrub dirt from the rocks. Wash the container and fill the bottom with 3 or 4 inches of potting soil.
Place the rocks on top of the soil. Plant the water plants in the soil, spacing them evenly in the container.
Decide where to put the water garden and move it to that place before filling the bowl with water. Then
fill with water.

After the container is filled with water, add the neutralizing solution in the amount indicated on the bottle.
Then watch your water garden grow! If you live in a dry, hot climate, be sure to give the garden water every
other day. Add more neutralizing solution every time you refill the bowl. Add fish or water snails to your
garden if you would like.

Horsetail.

Water iris.

Four-leaf
pennywort.

Greene & Greene lantern.

This is Mary Gamble playing in the pond at the Gamble House.

Mary's reflection in the water.

107

4 — West Grang View Hurff Home in Sierra Madre 1906 – 1921 & Caesar on front step

This is the house that Wendy Hurff grew up in.

Caesar, a dog, is on the front porch.

Memories of the Camp House

As I refelct back upon the wonderful years growing up in the Camp House, I realize how very special those memories are! Living in a wonderous home filled me with a sense of mystery, elegance, and excitement. I was eight years old when my family moved from a typical tract home to [Greene and Greene's] Camp House. It had not been occupied for months and months, making the structural woods extra creaky. The air was cool and damp and the aromas musty. It was wonderful! My mind stirred with fantasy and adventure. We spent weeks cleaning, airing out and exploring every nook and cranny of the old house.

One of my most memorable times was when my mother and I were dusting a little room under our magnificent stairway. The room had served past owners as a wine storage room. It was very cool and dark. As I dusted a wall, a hidden panel creaked open to reveal another dark cool space deep under the stairs. It was a secret room! We were at the same time surprised, delighted, and a little afraid. I ran for a flashlight.

Over the next weeks, the hidden room became our hideout. My brothers and I adorned the room with our secret treasures. We spent many happy hours there.

I consider my life truly blessed by having had the good fortune of growing up in a house with a rich sense of history, elegance, and beauty from the past. How lucky we were.

—Wendy Hurff

The Last Houses

By 1913, Charles Greene was tired and ready for a change. Work on the ultimate bungalow had worn him out. He wanted to spend more time painting and writing poems. In 1915, he took Alice and their five children on a camping trip to Northern California. The family fell in love with Carmel, a seaside village, and decided to move there. Eventually Charles withdrew his name from the architecture firm of Greene & Greene.

Alice and the children on a camping trip.

In Carmel, a man named D. L. James hired Charles to design a house overlooking the Pacific Ocean. The rocky cliff gave Charles the idea of building the James House with the jagged stones he found on the cliff. So Charles designed a house built from stones that looks like it grows out of the cliff. The house is not a structure standing on top of the cliff, but a continuation of the cliff in the shape of a house.

The ocean is down here.

The James House is on a cliff overlooking the Pacific Ocean.

When Charles and his family moved to Carmel, Henry, Emeline, and their four children remained in Pasadena. They lived in the large house Henry had designed for Emeline's mother, Charlotte Whitridge. Henry kept the architecture office open. He continued to design fine houses with Greene & Greene quality.

One of these houses, the Richardson House, has an extraordinary setting near California's central valley. This ranch house has views of distant mountains and is surrounded by orange groves. Henry designed the house to rest on a foundation of large stones—the same stones that dot the surrounding landscape. The Richardson House is built from adobe bricks that were made with the clay found on the ranch. Like the James House, the Richardson House rises up from its setting looking like a natural part of the countryside.

This is the Richardson House. Do you see the mountains in the distance?

At the end of their careers as architects, each brother built one last great house in California. Charles built the James House in Carmel and Henry built the Richardson House near Fresno. Each house was inspired by the natural beauty and the landscape of California. And each house was built from materials that blended into the surrounding countryside. These houses, and the houses that came before them, remain as monuments to the art and the craft of the Greene brothers who worked with hand and heart to create lasting beauty.

The picture on page 110 was taken from here.

This picture of the James House was taken from a helicopter.

LOOKING NORTH

ELEVATIONS OF M

INTERIOR ELEVATIONS

SCALE : ONE-QUARTER INCH EQUALS ONE FOOT.